local universes

nick allen

Maytree Press 2023

Published 2023 by Maytree Press

www.maytreepress.co.uk

ISBN: 978-1-913508-34-0

A CIP catalogue record of this book is available from the
British Library.

Cover: This Earth © David Coldwell

Author Photograph © Nick Allen

Maytree 044

Saltaire

we have the bend in the river
the long curve of the canal

and on a good day the air
smells of warm fruit loaf

local universes

for Dave,
because we all fucking miss you, that's why…

contents:

deerform

in the hoarfrost that knits the trees into a forest

a deer builds itself in my gaze   a deer building itself

in light   arriving with the drysnap of morning

building the light of itself from the sable undergrowth

the wilderness of the creature builds itself across

the soft morning of my gaze   our joined breath

the other river above that which flows itself light

over undergrowth   sable and deerform   my eyes

blink and in that moments unseeing   I am gone

hill fog

walking the loose cross-stitch / of tracks that mesh this hillside

pushing through the seaweed / heavy cling of bracken

a jogger emerges from mist / disappears as if pulled under

I pull my low-brow cap / down against the rain

shoulder my dark bulk / over the hill and startle

a nervous woman walking / a nervous dog pulling

muscles tense as whips / tight under soft pelt

my nodded greeting falls / against a lycra-clad back

a pair of sheep watch me / from here I can see the street

next to the street I live on / haul itself out the other side

deep time in hill fog

the moor under fog   an expanse of unmanaged time
I am lost and I am late   without a clock to chide me

shuffling across ghosts of mountains past   knowing I stand
on the ruins of something that once was even more astonishing

we navigate our histories as we have learned
to interpret landscapes   through what is absent

we see the gaps where something magnificent might have been
I mark the roughness of tracks in place of the precision of hours

so disorientated that I come upon a younger
version of myself   searching for north

looking for the steady hand of the compass   trying
to avoid the edge of the plateau   the sheer drop

a lapwing feather for Andrea Arnold
(after watching her reimagining of Wuthering Heights)

unbaptised and unsaved   alone before moors
before rain   I hand you a lapwing feather

we go lamping through mire and bog
where moss is king   we carry our love

as the torch carries its flame and we bear
our passion as the forge bears its heat

there are horses up here that will not be tamed
yet by the rod my brought-in-brother you will be taught

I kissed your scars and made you cry

in all that rain you held the horses long throat
at the laying down of our father   the young seriousness

on your face   buried deep and ferocious
in all that rain you were gone into night

you left me   crow alone over the moors

9

near home

after a day-long walk we dropped into a field we knew
to be near home   dropped over the fence and into the field

we found a loose assemblage of horses milling at their cropping
horses look like gravity   a permanence on the land

unconcerned   simply being   until they scent the dog
their stir and flight breeds a weightlessness at the sight

of them   giving lie to the thud and effort across the land
having raised up they would not settle   so we add

grudging yards around three sides of the square
ourselves as shield to the dog all the way to the stile

August evening reading
Kristín Ómarsdóttir

when the furious drum of a summer day
has finished with its beating and you can
bear to sit outside in the quiet and relative
cool   when the silkrip screech of birds
overhead tears your eye from the surreal
Icelandic melancholy to the soft yellow

blue above   to follow the peerless aeronautics
of the perpetual swift   the slice and carve
of their life and you watch to burn the memory
in case this is their last evening before May

from here   underlit contrails lead south over
sun-crazed uplands   the hunger of wildlife
shy riverbeds crackling their thirst   the great
sadnesses of this scorched mismanaged land

ten minutes on Midland Hill

looking out over Aldi waiting
for doors to open   people in cars

all messaging on devices
will we lose the power of speech

under a bright but gentle sun
a woman emerges from blankets

nestled between dumpsters
round the back of the shops

she stretches and half-heartedly
roots through the nearest bin

from the tallest chimney
a falcon scans the valley morning

park

only seven or eight years   in a frilly white skirt
and pink wellingtons   the girl studiously dribbles
a full-size football across the cricket field   with all

the concentration of Matthews or Eddie Gray
luring in the full back   waiting for that misstep
when they shift their weight the wrong way

like that famous photograph of Maradona
and the line of nervous Belgians   she cuts
a swathe through the gulls   unzipping them
from the shorn grass   they peel away to settle

and delicately fold into themselves   figurines
arranged on the unreliable mantel of the river
which I have seen   lift itself across the steppes
of these fields   flooding cafes   felling trees

bright yellow flowers

tied to a hardwood bench
rain-lashed   sleet-waiting

under a concrete sky
at the edge of a mud-soaked lawn

an old stone terrace   washed
with the light of February

even in this longest winter
twenty-nine is no age at all

close to home

in the early hours
of a non-descript night
somebody threw
an incendiary device

the fire burnt hard
and the fire burnt fast
at the heart of the flames
a rage burned black

in the first light
the house still stood
walls leaned erratic
but the house still stood

incomprehensible ash
covering everything

Heptonstall twice

there are two churchyards in Heptonstall
that I know of   one with foxgloves
and no corner for the devil
and the other one

there are two poets buried in Heptonstall
that I know of   one who declared themself
foolish enough to have been a poet
and the other one

no corner for the devil
(Heptonstall Methodist Church)

foxgloves in the churchyard
a poison that can
slow the heart rate   also

known as dead-mans bells
they can cause vomiting
diarrhoea and weight-loss

dilated pupils   hallucinations
yellow vision and halos
drooling   tremors   epilepsy

cardiac arrhythmia   seizures
delirium or death
also called witches gloves

17

weight

asked at the door of a chapel
to help with the carrying of a coffin
when I was a younger man
and my shoulders were still round
and I had not learnt the secret
of carrying the weight of others

at the door of the chapel
I shuffled my feet and looked
at the dust I stirred   and the
asker waited on my answer
until I said that I did not think
I could help bear the weight

of my cousin   himself barely
a man and too young in my mind
to be in need of my help
to get into this wretched place

years later and my shoulders
are broader my back straighter
but in truth I still do not feel
that I am strong enough

outwards everywhere
(i.m. Pat)

i

clouds squat fat and angry
on shadow-black peat moors

a congregation of wind-blown horses
gathers in a corner of a drystone field

nervously glancing about themselves
they stand on an edge of something

ii

at the river we are met by ducks
a family still in the re-making   skittering
on the surface trying to avoid collision

swallows   martens and swifts
all sip the air in their dash
grace burning their quick path

iii

huddled on the bank of the never-be-still
we let you go with petals
and small paper boats the children made

the river accepts you with less of a rush
more of a sigh   and from here
will carry you outwards   everywhere

a brief flurry   like your laughter
before the unstill river carries you
outwards always everywhere

heron in the rain

i

although the river is a dry throat
struggling to hold its own note

the note of its own song
struggling to hold the note

although the level is low
the river is a dry throat

river holds just enough
of itself to lip over the weir

ii

a heron under branches
is a pensioner at a bus stop

waterproof shrugging off rain
standing at the bus stop

the heron is a pensioner
waterproof under branches

above the unreliable mirror
feet above feet above feet

ripple

the sun is already down
the sky is not yet dark

when I lob the fallen
branch end over end

cabering into water
the slow river below

a stand of stark trees
and a flicked blanket

of crows lift out of their
almost imperceptible

roosts   concentrically
whirling in the gloom

above the pushed air
of the liquid sound

above the slapped
water of the plosion

the grey murder rises
into featureless silence

circling an evening
in search of its echo

ripple II

most people slip under
without too much fuss
as the world carries on

some ruffle the surface
maybe cause a pause
a moments reflection

yet others just stop us
they just stop us dead
in our shuffling tracks

and a few set off such
a tremor   such a wave
that we are swept away

helpless   lucky to ever
be set back on our feet

autumn prompt

unbidden and unavoidable   fresh as spring
autumn nests in the crooks of the branches
of trees across the way   ready to shake
off the weight of summer foliage   to bloom
that searing brown   a vibrato in red-and-
yellow   the comforting inferno of retrenchment

air becomes less substantial   wind rises
and falls as if breathing has rediscovered
itself   birds gather their force-fed young
committing to memory the star-lit path
of the first flight   to return next summer
to the maddening heave and rattle of it

on stillness

it is cold outside   some flakes drift from the afternoon
grey sky   the canal is a beaten panel of pewter
dented   as if a ball-peen hammer has been used
erratically across its surface   a lone swan shuffles
on dry land   scratched winter trees   stand thin

we are on our way to your funeral   it is unearthly
to think of you as still   as stopped   I cant make
the knowledge sit alongside the disbelief   you
were never still even when you were sat   always
one more hill to climb   one more tale to be told

approaching twilight on the old metal footbridge near Hirst Lock

in the uplands   the rain of days has gathered itself
and is pushing the young river   reckless with momentum

through the valley   I think back upstream   and remember
the river unspooling towards me   brash and awkward   shouldering

under the bat-roost aqueduct   where childhood toys hang tight
as morsels   there is a gently crook-ed elbow at the rowing club

four herons and fifty gulls walk the length of a new ploughed field
as if it were a crime scene   a cormorant fishes the silence

out of the Aire   how young water dimples sensuous
in its skin before the short chaos of the weir   a heron

drags the last prehistoric shadow of the ebbing day and
I am almost too slow to catch the electric now of the kingfisher

if only the poem would pick up

in this world   I am always so tired that
poetry seems the most distant thing

yet   when I make myself engage with it
actually write   it does feel better

whether or not the poem has a future
is entirely something other   right now

lets just settle for getting something down
we can worry about whether it is any good

later   and while I love the idea that other people
are doing their wonderful thing   I dont feel

celebratory   instead I just pass along to the next
and the next   there is so much of everything out there

but how much of it actually stops us   arrests us
like the first time you saw a Van Gogh in the flesh

or heard Lanegan sing   right now this babbling
stream of consciousness is what I am reduced to

and thinking on that breath-taking poem   when
the poet sat in front of a painting in a (Belgian?) gallery

looking out my study window where the moor
has almost completely been swallowed by clouds

I watch snow falling against blacker trees   the roofs
of the houses nearby are wet and white   and it is pretty

there are brief crows   it is pretty but it feels like stasis
like hanging on the phone for a call that wont connect

last poem of the year

frost holds all that tussocky grass in thrall to the morning
as if it were a stopped sea
time nestled in each crystal waiting release
mud is thin-iced and crackling under boot
a resting dog raises a paw out of snow as it looks around
wishing it could chase those squirrels
in the tree-tops bare against a tea-light sun
a thin dog made of little but elastic and balsawood
flashes from undergrowth and fails to parkour up a trunk in pursuit
the high branches still sleeved in snow
as when a loved one lays their hand gently across the arm of another
untidy family groups call other dogs
and encourage toddlers with promises of sweets back at the car
and we sit
shivering our last nip on the starlit backstep
in the minutes before bed never to know
if we are the galaxies other gazers are looking at

and will they still be soft these times   will these hours yet be gentle

last night   as we were going to bed
you looked out of the window
at what had been driving rain
you said   it is turning to snow

for several moments we watched
as the drops became heavy
wet flakes drifting more than falling
across the streetlight

each of us silently wondering
if it would settle by morning

these hours

when nights sweet flight is snagged
and comes to rest in the doldrums

those barely spoken of but impossible
to ignore hours when we have the world
to ourselves and our irrational thoughts

that cause such a ruckus and storm
when next door is as close as you and

as far away   and the hours will not
march on but stagger back and forth
an uncooperative drunk   and my mouth

is dry

and they are finding atrocities   torture
mass murder and unmarked graves

in neighbours gardens   these are
Kaminskys waiting hours   harrowed by war
the possibility of cancer   still no word

another round

(i.m. Dave Dowden, aka. "Lid")

two men in a pub   both aware that they are dying
one in that vague from-the-moment-we-are-born kind of way

the other because a specialist has told him to think in months
rather than years   they recall paths   steep up the sides of mountains

how they can give on to bright sunshine   banks of cloud   sometimes
a shimmering tarn   the worn-rock track up the broken tooth

of Pen-y-Ghent   how on a clear day from the flat-top of Ingleborough
you can see much of northern England   the bay at Morecambe

Silverdale   they remember night games made brilliant
by gigantic sunflower floodlights   anticipation at turnstiles

the fortnightly manifestation of hope over experience   days
when parking cost a pork-pie   the art of goal-hanging   the importance

of the square ball across the box and singing the praises
of Bielsa the Redeemer   those promotion afternoons with the big screen

in the big garden and all those big hearts   the women they love
and who love them in their turn   and they sit in this hilltop pub

looking down the valley at the path they have taken
they know that if all of this is not about love then it is about nothing
at all   and they drink another round to the sheer gentle joy of it

a poem originally titled *unprecedented* when written three years ago but which will be known from here on in as *an unprecedented opportunity missed* or *the poem formerly known as unprecedented*

let us take no more interest in stocks and shares
profit margins or exchange rates

lets bake a huge cake and leave it
on a neighbours doorstep

let us sing the praises of nurses and doctors
shelf-stackers and the delivery guys

lets hear no more about the rich and famous
they can look after themselves

let us play with kittens or walk our dogs
stand under a newly budding tree

lets talk with a stranger and share the last
two packets in the supermarket

let us hook up social media and Skype
the friend we know who lives alone

lets for once and all put love ahead of money
planet before profit   the many before the few

let us be that stranger offering kindness

the city is learning to breathe again
songbirds chorus the bus route
in Venice the canals run clear
and are home once more to fish

stormclouds

the clotting fills the horizon like cholesterol

big hot drops of rain make the shape of a car

in the car-still night where lights bounce to prove

the darkness   enormous across the skies

like freight trains   cargo ships rolling the seven

midnight seas   full of the weight of themselves

and their purpose upon Earth unseen by all

but stars   into this world of apertures darkness

slips unnoticed   and this colossal rain that came

and came again with all the urgency of being

acknowledgements

deerform was previously published in Poetry Scotland

and will they still be soft these times   will these hours yet be gentle was previously published in the Seconds Anthology

Morag Anderson, Helen Mort & Matt Nicholson have offered opinions on one or more of these poems: I am grateful for their time, brilliance and willingness to rein me in when needed.